THE TROUBLE WITH JESUS

BIBLE STUDY

THE TROUBLE WITH JESUS

BIBLE STUDY

JOSEPH M. STOWELL

WITH MARK TOBEY

Contents

FIRST THOUGHTS ON HOW TO BEGIN

Christians in the first century knew well the costs of following Jesus. Thousands suffered brutal persecution, countless others were imprisoned, and many were martyred.

What bound them together was an unswerving resolve to align themselves with the name of Christ as Messiah—the Savior of the world. In a time of religious pluralism where all gods had equal playing time, holding an exclusive claim came at a heavy price.

Sound familiar?

If you've read *The Trouble With Jesus,* you've already made the connection. In America, most Christians haven't suffered yet to the point of shedding blood for His name, but those days may not be far off. Still, the challenges of following Christ and contending for Him are intense. After the terrorist attacks of September 11, 2001, many people regained a sense of religious awareness. Folks talked openly about praying for loved ones and for the country. Mainline churches noticed marked increases in worship attendance and ministry involvement.

Dignitaries and politicians invoked God's name at public gatherings. Still, God may be "in," but Jesus is "out." Religion makes sense in desperate and uncertain times . . . but any exclusive claim to truth sets off alarms.

So how should Christians respond? Do you and I keep Jesus to ourselves to avoid conflict with a culture that shows disdain for our deepest convictions? Didn't Jesus say His children were to be peacemakers and show love to those who oppose us? Does the Bible offer practical guidance on how to stand for Jesus in today's confused and broken world? What can you and I learn from those courageous believers who were part of the early church?

We'll explore the answers to those questions and many more like them in this study. This is an interactive study that provides opportunities for you to record your thoughts and create discussion among a group. Before going through each chapter in this study, read in advance the corresponding book chapter in *The Trouble With Jesus*. The chapter titles of the Study Guide match the titles in the book. The *Questions for Reflection* and *A Look at the Book* sections can be used either for individual study or as group discussion guides.

If you're studying as a group, you can use one chapter a week for an eight-week study. Designate someone to lead the discussion as group members share their reflections.

Following each chapter in the Study Guide, there will be *Action Points* designed to give you practical ways to apply what you've discovered.

You will need a Bible and something to write with, but, above all, the best preparation is to humble yourself before the Lord. Ask Him to speak to you and challenge you from His Word. He longs for you to deepen your resolve to follow Jesus and proclaim Him to

a disillusioned and increasingly frightened world. May you know
His grace and power as you do!

As you come to him, the living Stone—rejected by men but chosen by God and precious to him—you also, like living stones, are being built into a spiritual house to be a holy priesthood, offering spiritual sacrifices acceptable to God through Jesus Christ. For in Scripture it says:

"See, I lay a stone in Zion,
a chosen and precious cornerstone,
and the one who trusts in him
will never be put to shame."

Now to you who believe, this stone is precious.
But to those who do not believe,

"The stone the builders rejected
has become the capstone,"

and,

"A stone that causes men to stumble
and a rock that makes them fall."

They stumble because they disobey the message—
which is also what they were destined for.

But you are a chosen people, a royal priesthood, a holy nation, a people belonging to God, that you may declare the praises of him who called you out of darkness into his wonderful light . . . Live such good lives among the pagans that, though they accuse you of doing wrong, they may see your good deeds and glorify God on the day he visits us.

୬ 1 PETER 2:4–9, 12 ୬

CHAPTER ONE

BREAKFAST WITHOUT JESUS

The Traditions That Divide Us

You and I live in challenging days. Perhaps more than any other time in your lifetime, you sense the uneasiness that comes from knowing your religious beliefs represent a minority worldview. That Jesus is the only way rings not only unpopular but sounds bigoted and divisive.

Christianity and the values it represents have undergone intensifying assaults for generations—to the point where now in America and in Western Europe what remains is little more than a spiritual ground zero, a barren place of ruin and dismantled faith. We're suffering from its effects—the shock of being locked out of public schools, local and national political agendas, and being marginalized in our own communities. It's easy to wander aimlessly through the wreckage wondering what hit us.

"It was then [at the Chicago Leadership Prayer Breakfast] that I began to realize why Jesus was unwelcome. [The speaker] was telling us in no uncertain terms that an 'Only-Way-Jesus' didn't fit in the new religious order." —*The Trouble With Jesus*, 15.

But that's not what Christ has in mind for His people. Ours is to be a victorious experience that draws others to the Savior. Since the days of the early church, believers have confronted culture with the life-changing message of Christ and His love. Now is no time to shrink from that mission. But let's be honest: Resisting the temptation to soften our resolve drains us of energy and spirit.

?

Questions for Reflection

Take some time to think (or discuss as a group) about how today's world challenges your commitment to Jesus and His gospel. Record some thoughts in the spaces below.

Describe a situation where you felt uncomfortable because what you believe about Jesus didn't fit the majority. How did you respond?

_____

_____

In what ways do you feel society shows its disdain for Christ's exclusive claims? How about your personal faith?

_____

_____

How well prepared do you feel to meet the growing opposition to Christian values and claims?

_____

_____

So Much at Stake

The antidote to a shaky faith is to have beliefs grounded in the truths of God's Word. We need to build on the firm foundation of Scripture. To deny that Jesus is the only way is to reject the message of the Bible. Look, for instance, at the apostle Paul's magnificent words written to Christians struggling to keep their focus:

He (Jesus) is the image of the invisible God, the firstborn over all creation. For by him all things were created: things in heaven and on earth, visible and invisible, whether thrones or powers or rulers or authorities; all things were created by him and for him. He is before all things, and in him all things hold together. And he is the head of the body, the church; he is the beginning and the firstborn from among the dead, so that in everything he might have the supremacy. For God was pleased to have all his fullness dwell in him, and through him to reconcile to himself all things, whether things on earth or things in heaven, by making peace through his blood, shed on the cross.

⇝ COLOSSIANS 1:15–20

Based on this passage, how would you explain to someone in your own words who Jesus is and why you believe He is the only way to heaven?

_____

_____

_____

Go back through the verses and write down the words Paul uses to describe who Jesus is—His identity.

_____

_____

Write down the words and phrases that describe what He has done—His works.

_____

_____

How is it significant that Jesus is the visible image of an invisible God?

_____

_____

_____

What do you think Paul means when he writes that Jesus is "before all things" and in Him "all things hold together"? Do you live your life believing that?

_____

_____

In what ways does the fullness of God "dwell" in Jesus? Are there any other gods or religious leaders that make such claims to deity?

_____

_____

Using what you've discovered here, how would you address the common sentiment that "Jesus was a good moral teacher but not God"?

_____

_____

Write down (or discuss as a group) how today's society reacts to the truths about Jesus found in these verses.

_____

_____

Are you beginning to get the picture? That's the trouble with Jesus! The Bible makes it clear that Jesus is God and that He is the only way to eternal life.

A  at the BOOK

Think about how your life would be different if Jesus wasn't who He says He is and didn't do what He claims to have done. Read the following verses and write down how you would finish the sentence:

1 John 1:9   Without Him . . .

_____

_____

1 Timothy 2:5   Without Him . . .

_____

_____

Acts 4:12   Without Him . . .

_____

_____

John 14:14   Without Him . . .

_____

_____

John 15:11   Without Him . . .

_____

_____

Matthew 9:9   Without Him . . .

_____

_____

John 4:14   Without Him . . .

_____

_____

John 3:36   Without Him . . .

_____

_____

It's hard to imagine life without Christ, isn't it? Thankfully, God's Word assures you and me that Jesus is who He says He is and that He has provided a way for all people to know the peace of forgiveness and the promise of eternal life.

Now would be a good time to pause and thank the Lord for what He has done for you and for all that you have in Him. Take a few moments to pray right now (if you're in a small group, spend a few minutes praying together).

ACTION POINTS

⇨ Take some time over the next week to read the entire book of Colossians. You may need to read it a couple of times to begin to grasp its profound truths. When you read, ask the Lord to speak to you by His Spirit and to deepen your understanding of Christ and everything He has done for you.

⇨ Using the truths you've discovered and reflected on, write out your testimony explaining why you've put your faith in Jesus. Put your thoughts into your own words. Share what you've written with a close friend. Then ask the Lord to give you an opportunity to share your faith with someone who needs the Savior.

⇨ No doubt someone in your neighborhood, a colleague in your office, an employee in your business, or someone you connect with regularly embraces a religion other than Christianity. Maybe they are Muslim, Jewish, Hindu, or an atheist. Commit to pray for that person each day as you continue this study, asking the Lord to prepare him or her to hear the gospel. Ask God to help you begin a deeper relationship with that person. You might ask that individual to lunch or plan a time for your children to play together. Keep it low-key by simply offering kindness and friendship. Watch how the Lord works!

> Lord Jesus, thank You for making it so clear that You are the only way to eternal life. Help me to resist the temptation to simply go along with the crowd. Help me begin to really understand who You are and everything You have done for me. In Your name, Amen.

There came a man who was sent from God; his name was John. He came as a witness to testify concerning that light, so that through him all men might believe. He himself was not the light; he came only as a witness to the light. The true light that gives light to every man was coming into the world.

He was in the world, and though the world was made through him, the world did not recognize him. He came to that which was his own, but his own did not receive him. Yet to all who received him, to those who believed in his name, he gave the right to become children of God—children born not of natural descent, nor of human decision or a husband's will, but born of God.

The Word became flesh and made his dwelling among us. We have seen his glory, the glory of the One and Only, who came from the Father, full of grace and truth.

JOHN 1:6–14

CHAPTER TWO

DÉJÀ VU ALL OVER AGAIN

Jesus and the New Paganism

The Scriptures tell us that when Jesus came to the world, the world did not recognize Him. Even among His own people, the Jews, Jesus went unnoticed. At the time of Jesus' birth the world stood in a state of spiritual darkness. Yet the Jewish people still viewed their religious system as superior to the paganism of the day. The Jewish people served the living God, the Creator of the universe.

But, as the apostle John points out, when God chose to make His dwelling among us through His Son, His own people rejected Him. We shouldn't be surprised then that our own pagan culture turns its back on Him too.

When Christians started to preach and teach that Jesus was God and that He was the only way, the world, including the Jewish people, erupted in protest.

Sounds like déjà vu, all over again, doesn't it?

? Questions for Reflection

In what ways does present-day secular culture embrace their idea of God but reject Jesus?

_____

_____

_____

_____

What does it mean to have a secular society?

_____

_____

What are some examples of secular influence in the church?

_____

_____

_____

In what ways has the ministry of your church met resistance from the unbelieving community?

_____

_____

_____

Paganism allows your god as a preference but never as the singularly preeminent God. (*The Trouble With Jesus*, 35.)

Back to the Future

Believers in the early church also lived out their faith under the pressures of tolerance and paganism. Since the time of Abraham, God's people have lived among extreme religious groups known to worship strange gods and to practice bizzare religious rituals.

> The gods were amoral or, more often, immoral, granting their adherents license for unrestrained sensual fulfillment. The preeminent goddess of the first century was Artemis, who represented virginity and motherhood. Her temples were filled with prostitutes who serviced her followers on demand. Since the transition from virginity to motherhood was consummated at intercourse, the act was celebrated as an act of worship and an expression of loyalty to the goddess. Believers who lived pure and chaste lives were disdained. After all, who would want to worship a god like theirs? A god so limiting and oppressive? *(The Trouble With Jesus, 40).*

A great spiritual darkness during the time of Christ and the beginning of the church kept many people blind to the truth. That same spiritual darkness that was present then now hangs like an ominous cloud over our world today. Notice the role darkness played in Christ's first coming to earth:

> *In the beginning was the Word, and the Word was with God, and the Word was God. He was with God in the beginning. Through him all things were made; without him nothing was made that has been made. In him was life, and that life was the light of men. The light shines in the darkness, but the darkness has not understood it. There came a man who was sent from God; his name was John. He came as a witness to testify concerning that light, so that through him all men might believe. He himself was not the light; he came only as a witness to the light. The true light that gives light to every man was coming into the world.*
> — JOHN 1:1–9

The apostle John, the writer of the words you just read, tells us that Jesus, the Word, is God. He was with God at creation and there's nothing in this world that came into being without His power. And that same Word, Jesus, came as light into a spiritually dark world.

What is a spiritual darkness?

_____

_____

In what way did Jesus coming to earth bring light?

_____

_____

According to these verses, why did the people of the world reject the darkness?

_____

_____

Has anything changed about how the world responds today to the light of Jesus? Why or why not?

_____

_____

A LOOK at the BOOK

Matthew 1:22–23

What do these verses reveal about the nature of Jesus' advent?

_____

_____

_____

What is the meaning and significance of His name, Immanuel, especially in a culture of secularism and paganism?

_____

_____

_____

Matthew 5:14–16

According to this passage how are Christians to live in the world?

_____

_____

_____

John 15:18–19

Why does the world "hate" followers of Christ? Why are we surprised when others react negatively to our beliefs?

_____

_____

_____

Philippians 1:27

What does Paul encourage Christians to do? Why would we want to do this?

_____

_____

_____

1 Peter 2:12

What concerned Peter about the believers to which he wrote?

_____

_____

_____

Christians in the early church understood the need to live honorably before the Lord and the unbelieving world. They anticipated persecution and opposition because Jesus and the apostles had prepared them for it. Yet, in spite of the peril, they lived for and proclaimed the name of Jesus boldly. No doubt there were few weak-hearted believers in that day.

How different this is from our world. As Christians, we insist on such little distinctions between our lives and the lives of unbelievers. In fact, apart from seeing that we attend regular Sunday services, unbelievers might be hard-pressed to notice anything about us that's genuinely different.

Perhaps the Lord has begun to show you areas in your life that don't honor Him. Those are areas He wants you to confess and ultimately surrender to Him.

ACTIONPOINTS

⇨ Write down an area of your life you sense is displeasing to Him. There may be more than one. Take time to confess that to Him and ask Him for forgiveness.

⇨ Think about some simple ways you can live out your faith and demonstrate God's love among your neighbors. Invite some neighbors for a backyard cookout or dessert and coffee. Reach out to a local retirement center or nursing home and offer to spend time talking with and encouraging residents. Volunteer to tutor underprivileged children in your community.

⇨ Consider starting a unique ministry with a group of people in your church, such as a ministry of compassion to AIDS patients or unwed mothers and their families.

Dear Lord, teach me to obey You regardless of what You ask me to do. More than anything, I want the people around me to see You and become convinced You are the answer to all of their needs. In Your name, Amen.

Blessed are the poor in spirit,
for theirs is the kingdom of heaven,
Blessed are those who mourn,
for they will be comforted.
Blessed are the meek,
for they will inherit the earth.
Blessed are those who hunger
and thirst for righteousness,
for they will be filled.
Blessed are the merciful,
for they will be shown mercy.
Blessed are the pure in heart,
for they will see God.
Blessed are the peacemakers,
for they will be called sons of God.
Blessed are those who are
persecuted because of righteousness,
for theirs is the kingdom of heaven.

❧ MATTHEW 5:3–10 ❧

CHAPTER THREE

TERMS OF ENGAGEMENT
Salt and Light in Action

Our world has witnessed a remarkable surge of interest in spiritual matters. Americans for the most part seem strangely at ease discussing matters of faith and life and death in places ranging from living rooms to teachers' lounges to locker rooms to cable talk shows. Everyone from Larry King to Katie Couric to Jay Leno to Oprah has gone out of the way to invite God onto center stage.

Lisa Beamer inspired a nation as she spoke courageously and tenderly in interview after interview about her husband's brave attempt to rescue the dozens of passengers on a United Airlines jetliner overtaken by a small band of terrorists on September 11, 2001. Each time, the world listened in awe as she described a quiet, confident trust in God that gave her beloved Todd the resolve to act.

Christians cheered. Unbelievers wept in sympathy. Her bold witness moved us all.

"On the platform of great personal tragedy, the kind that would normally overwhelm non-Jesus people with deep despair and hopelessness, Lisa proved that Jesus works even in the worst of times. The 'good works' of unflinching trust and confidence caught the attention of a watching world . . . in Jesus' terms, it was salt and light in action."—*The Trouble With Jesus*, 49-50.

But do we have to experience horrific tragedy in our lives to be motivated to represent our faith in God?

Questions
for
Reflection

Why does it sometimes take painful circumstances to cause us to evaluate and rely on our faith to see us through them?

_____

_____

_____

_____

What other examples of a salt-and-light faith has the secular media put on display?

_____

_____

Why do you think those stories matter to the world?

_____

_____

_____

Can you describe other experiences where some individual spoke boldly about his or her faith in Jesus after a crisis?

_____

_____

_____

What impression did that have on you and/or others?

_____

_____

Still, Jesus wants us to express our love for Him in our everyday experiences as well. Most of us will never get an opportunity to testify to what Jesus has done in our lives on national television. But every day we do have occasions to be salt and light. Take a few minutes to study and reflect on the following passages of Scripture.

A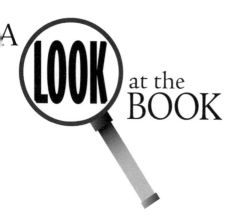

Matthew 5:13–20

What is the context of the verses?

_____

_____

_____

_____

To whom was Jesus speaking?

_____

_____

_____

_____

In what ways are the virtues Jesus mentions in Matthew 5:3–12, the Beatitudes, practical applications for being salt and light?

_____

_____

_____

Matthew 5 and 6

Write down character traits or actions that Jesus said would be evident in the life of a genuine believer. (For instance, in Matthew 5:23–24, Jesus teaches that Christians don't hold grudges, and they do whatever it takes to reconcile with others.)

_____

_____

_____

_____

If Christians today obeyed Jesus' words and lived according to these verses today, how would culture be impacted?

_____

_____

_____

In what ways would unbelievers be forced to acknowledge Jesus and His followers?

_____

_____

_____

ACTIONPOINTS

Beginning on page 56 in *The Trouble With Jesus*, there is a section called "Out of the Salt Shaker . . . Out from Under the Bushel!"

In that section you may recall the challenge to get "beyond ourselves" and begin impacting the world around us by the way we represent Jesus. The chapter ends listing several pitfalls that hinder the "salt-and-light" effect we Christians can have on culture. Reread each category and write down some ways that you might fall prey to these traps.

The problem of:

⇨assimilation _____

⇨isolation _____

⇨cloistering _____

⇨correctness _____

⇨confrontation _____

⇨compromise _____

> Lord Jesus, show me ways that I can be salt and light to my world in this day. Point out areas in my life where I am hiding Your light under a bushel, rather than letting You shine. For the sake of Your kingdom, Amen.

Men of Israel, listen to this: Jesus of Nazareth was a man accredited by God to you by miracles, wonders and signs, which God did among you through him, as you yourselves know. This man was handed over to you by God's set purpose and foreknowledge; and you, with the help of wicked men, put him to death by nailing him to the cross. But God raised him from the dead, freeing him from the agony of death, because it was impossible for death to keep its hold on him . . .

≈ ACTS 2:22–24 ≈

CHAPTER FOUR

JESUS IN THE NO-SPIN ZONE

Commitment 1:
Declaration . . . Speaking Up for Jesus

Most people understand the power of words. Words have started wars, incited riots, impelled citizens to rebel, and inspired a generation to vote. Words can be equally powerful for good and for evil. But in these days when so much is at stake for Christians, this is no time to clam up and be silent. Unless Christians speak up for the real Jesus, others will speak for us and twist Him into something He's not, minimizing His power and message.

"Making Jesus fit is a problem. For Him to fit [in today's culture of religious tolerance], you have to twist and disfigure Jesus in serious ways. In order to become all things to all people, Jesus must be spun as not having said what the Bible affirms He said. A one-size-fits-all Jesus must be tolerant of everyone, judgmental toward none, kind but not analytical, loving but not disciplining, a moldable figment of every imagination, a bland, almost boring, inoffensive, nondivisive, disposable Jesus."
—*The Trouble With Jesus*, 80.

Questions
for
Reflection

How have Christians responded to challenges by the culture? In what ways can we fail in our responsibility to speak boldly for Jesus?

_____

_____

_____

In your opinion, what is really at stake if Christians don't respond to such assault with clarity and boldness?

_____

_____

_____

How prepared do you feel to speak the truth about Jesus when faced with a challenge to your faith?

_____

_____

Jesus in the No-Spin Zone

Believers throughout the first century kept the message of who He is clear. Many paid the ultimate price for their bold words in defense of Jesus. To the watching world, Christ's followers were marked by a firm resolve to follow and speak up for Him no matter the cost. Hebrews 11 ends with words of honor and praise for Christians who were willing to suffer mind-boggling consequences for their faith.

The point is that if Christians don't speak up for Jesus, the world will spin Him into something He's not. That's too big a risk.

Christians must be committed to knowing what the Bible teaches about who Jesus is and why He came. A passage from Paul's letter to the Philippian believers strikes at the heart of Christ's identity and mission. Read through the following verses and reflect on the questions that follow.

> *Your attitude should be the same as that of Christ Jesus:*
> *Who, being in very nature God, did not consider equality with God something to be grasped, but made himself nothing, taking the very nature of a servant, being made in human likeness. And being found in appearance as a man, he humbled himself and became obedient to death—even death on a cross!*
> *Therefore God highly exalted him to the highest place and gave him the name that is above every name, that at the name of Jesus every knee should bow, in heaven and on earth and under the earth, and every tongue confess that Jesus Christ is Lord, to the glory of God the Father.*
> ⇝ PHILIPPIANS 2:5–11

How does this passage defend His deity and His humanity?

_____

_____

_____

What aspects of His character does Paul mention in these verses?

_____

_____

_____

According to this passage what was Christ's mission? How did He accomplish it on earth?

_____

_____

_____

What is the significance of God exalting Jesus? Who or what are typically exalted over Jesus in society? What is the significance of the declaration that someday all the universe will bow down and extol His name?

_____

_____

_____

_____

How can these truths give us boldness to speak up for Jesus in a culture that challenges who He truly is?

_____

_____

"In times like these, knowing *what to do* begins with knowing *what is true about Jesus* and making sure that there is not the slightest erosion. We must know that He is God, as He claimed to be. That He is the only way. That His death on Calvary finished the work of salvation. That all who come, apart from any work or merit and regardless of class, culture, or color, will be welcomed as His child. That He rose from the dead as final proof that He had conquered death and sin and hell. That He is coming again. That He will judge the world." —*The Trouble With Jesus*, 81.

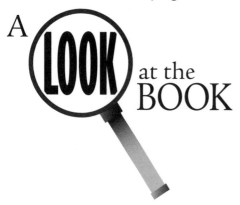

A **LOOK** at the **BOOK**

Look up the following passages of Scripture. After each one, write a word or two about what the verse(s) teach about Jesus Christ.

Micah 5:2

_____

_____

Isaiah 9:6

_____

John 1:1, 14

_____

John 8:58

_____

Colossians 1:16

_____

1 Peter 2:21

_____

Hebrews 10:1–10

_____

Galatians 4:4

_____

Hebrews 4:15

_____

Matthew 16:16

_____

Revelation 19:16

_____

Matthew 28:18

_____

Matthew 20:28; 1 Timothy 2:6

_____

2 Corinthians 5:18–19

_____

2 Corinthians 5:21

_____

John 20:11–17

_____

John 14:6–7

_____

The truths about Jesus found in the Bible are inexhaustible. And as Christians, we are called to spend our lives pursuing Christ and knowing Him. But knowledge alone can lead us to pride. The knowledge we gain as a result of seeking Him ought to transform us and make us more and more like Him. Only then will we be able to speak up for Him with power and conviction.

ACTIONPOINTS

⇨ Discuss some ways you believe you can "speak up for Jesus." For instance, "represent Him at a school board meeting or in a town council meeting."

⇨ Get together with a small group of believers and pray specifically for the pastors in your area, that they would be bold in the opportunities they have to speak up for Jesus.

⇨ When you pray, ask God for courage and faith to speak boldly for Jesus when opportunities arise.

Dear God, thank You for Your Word that speaks plainly and boldly about Jesus Christ. Show me ways to proclaim those truths with boldness and grace to a world so desperately in need of You.
In Jesus' name, Amen.

You are the light of the world. A city on a hill cannot be hidden. Neither do people light a lamp and put it under a bowl. Instead they put it on its stand, and it gives light to everyone in the house. In the same way, let your light shine before men, that they may see your good deeds and praise your Father in heaven.

≫ MATTHEW 5:14–16 ≪

CHAPTER FIVE

JESUS IN THE SPOTLIGHT

Commitment 2:
Demonstration ... Showing Up for Jesus

You and I live in a very different world than that of our parents and grandparents. The old saying "Times have changed" certainly rings true in most of our minds. In one sense, people appear more open to considering spiritual things than they were a generation ago. Yet, at the same time, there is a segment of our culture that flat-out opposes anything religious—and especially any religion that claims exclusivity.

Gone are the days when evangelistic rallies and gospel crusades enjoy remarkable effectiveness. Organizations like Campus Crusade for Christ and Youth for Christ used to be welcomed with open arms on secular high school and university campuses. Today they are challenged and face unique, and sometimes strident, opposition.

The direct approach to sharing Jesus with non-Jesus people worked a generation ago. But, as we've already mentioned, "times have changed."

"My father and grandfather preached into a culture that shared a basic intellectual acceptance to the claims of Jesus. People in their churches found that witnessing for Jesus at work or in their neighborhood at least had the advantage of a general cultural awareness of God, Jesus, sin, heaven, and hell. In their world, hostility to the gospel was much more subdued. In those days people were more willing to listen to truths about Jesus and His claims . . . For us it is different. As Dorothy said to her dog in the *Wizard of Oz,* "Toto, I don't think we're in Kansas anymore." Taking Jesus to the hearts of a needy world is more complicated in our times. The resistance is more intense."—*The Trouble With Jesus,* 89–90.

Questions for Reflection

Take some time to think about and write down how culture today resists the message of Christ.

_____

_____

_____

_____

_____

In what ways have you personally been affected by opposition to Christianity?

_____

_____

_____

How have values changed from a generation or two ago? In what ways do those changing values impact the church?

_____

_____

_____

Good for Nothing . . . Good for Something

God has always expected His people, the people of faith, to represent Him in a world that rejects His initiatives. Clearly, in our day, words alone will not be enough to capture the attention and respect of an increasingly secular world. We have to impact our world not only by what we say—*declaration*—but also in how we live—*demonstration*.

God's Word sets a standard for all of us, showing us the way to be "in the world, but not of it." The New Testament speaks comprehensively to our need as believers to "show up" for Jesus in a non-Jesus world. But the Old Testament does as well. Read through Psalm 1, written first to God's chosen people of Israel, as a guide for living for Him in a godless culture.

> *Blessed is the man who does not walk in the counsel of the wicked or stand in the way of sinners or sit in the seat of mockers. But his delight is in the law of the* LORD, *and on his law he meditates day and night. He is like a tree planted by streams of water, which yields its fruit in season and whose leaf does not wither. Whatever he does prospers.*
>
> *Not so the wicked! They are like chaff that the wind blows away. Therefore the wicked will not stand in the judgment, nor sinners in the assembly of the righteous.*
>
> *For the* LORD *watches over the way of the righteous, but the way of the wicked will perish.*
>
> ꙮ PSALM 1

There are only 121 English words in that entire psalm, yet those few words lay down a life plan of blessing for the child of God who wants to "show up" for Him in a lost world.

What do you believe to be the main purpose of this psalm?
What kinds of people are compared?

_____

_____

How does the writer of this psalm use images from nature to make those comparisons?

_____

_____

God, through the words of David, promises blessing to the godly and judgment for the wicked. Blessing comes from taking delight in the principles and promises of God's Word, the law. Let's apply the words of this psalm to the Christian life.

What is the first step we need to take to demonstrate our allegiance to Jesus in a non-Jesus world?

_____

_____

What does God promise us if we take Him at His Word and obey His commands no matter what the cost?

_____

_____

_____

I think we all understand that showing up for Jesus in the way we live does not simply mean keeping all the rules. That on its own can lead us down a slippery path toward legalism and hypocrisy. Rather, Jesus wants us to move beyond just doing what's proper to a life that draws others to Him. That takes transformation!

A LOOK at the BOOK

Reread pages 95–101 in *The Trouble With Jesus.* Notice the two Greek words that the New Testament uses for *being good.* Those two words are (1) *agathos,* which has to do with moral uprightness, respectable character, and honesty; and (2) *kalos*, the most commonly used word in the New Testament, which has to do with actions and motives that impact others for good.

Agathos: **Character that is good, morally upright, and respectable**
Kalos: **Doing good deeds**

Read the passages below and circle the kind(s) of goodness depicted. Some may refer to both types.

> 1 CORINTHIANS 6:18–20: *Flee from sexual immorality. All other sins a man commits are outside his body, but he who sins sexually sins against his own body. Do you not know that your body is a temple of the Holy Spirit, who is in you, whom you have received from God? You are not your own; you were bought with a price. Therefore honor God with your body.*
>
> AGATHOS   KALOS
>
> _____
>
> _____

> 1 PETER 1:14–16: *As obedient children, do not conform to the evil desires you had when you lived in ignorance. But just as he who called you is holy, so be holy in all you do; for it is written: "Be holy, because I am holy."*
>
> AGATHOS   KALOS
>
> _____
>
> _____

> 1 PETER 2:11–12: *Dear friends, I urge you, as aliens and strangers in the world, to abstain from sinful desires, which war against your soul. Live such good lives among the pagans that, though they accuse you of doing wrong, they may see your good deeds and glorify God on the day he visits us.*

AGATHOS   **K**ALOS

_____

_____

1 THESSALONIANS 4:3–6: *It is God's will that you should be sanctified: that you should avoid sexual immorality; that each of you should learn to control his own body in a way that is holy and honorable, not in passionate lust like the heathen, who do not know God; and that in this matter no one should wrong his brother or take advantage of him.*

AGATHOS   **K**ALOS

_____

_____

1 THESSALONIANS 4:11–12: *Make it your ambition to lead a quiet life, to mind your own business and to work with your hands, just as we told you, so that your daily life may win the respect of outsiders and so that you will not be dependent on anybody.*

AGATHOS   **K**ALOS

_____

_____

GALATIANS 6:9–10: *Let us not become weary in doing good, for at the proper time we will reap a harvest if we do not give up. Therefore, as we have opportunity, let us do good to all people, especially to those who belong to the family of believers.*

AGATHOS   **K**ALOS

_____

_____

ACTIONPOINTS

⇨ Begin praying each day that God would show you areas of your life where you are not demonstrating holiness. Go back through the verses you've looked at in this chapter and see if there are things you know God is displeased with.

⇨ Make a list of people you know in your community who have special needs: lonely elderly folks in a resident care facility, a family with a special-needs child, a person with AIDS, or some troubled youth. Ask God to show you ways you can reach out to them that will demonstrate both kinds of goodness that we've studied.

⇨ Ask God to show you specific ways of "showing up" for Jesus through your words *and* your actions.

> Lord, thank You for these challenging truths that You are teaching me. I thank You that You have made the power to live a good life and do good deeds available to me. Give me a compassionate heart for my neighbors. In Jesus' name, Amen.

In reply Jesus said: "A man was going down from Jerusalem to Jericho, when he fell into the hands of robbers. They stripped him of his clothes, beat him and went away, leaving him half dead. A priest happened to be going down the same road, and when he saw the man, he passed by on the other side. So too, a Levite, when he came to the place and saw him, passed by on the other side. But a Samaritan, as he traveled, came where the man was; and when he saw him, he took pity on him. He went to him and bandaged his wounds, pouring on oil and wine. Then he put the man on his own donkey, took him to an inn and took care of him. The next day he took out two silver coins and gave them to the innkeeper. 'Look after him,' he said, 'and when I return, I will reimburse you for any extra expense you may have.'

Which of these three do you think was a neighbor to the man who fell into the hands of robbers?"

LUKE 10:30–36

CHAPTER SIX

JESUS TO THE NEEDY

Commitment 3:
Compassion . . . Reaching Out for Jesus

The events of 9/11 remain forever etched in the minds of all who witnessed them. The grim scenes at ground zero, at the burned out Pentagon wing, and in a scorched field in rural Pennsylvania remind us all that evil really does exist in this world.

The heroes of 2001 were the nameless firefighters, rescue workers, doctors, nurses, police officers, and countless volunteers that spent days on end sifting through the carnage in search of survivors and remains of loved ones. Their remarkable bravery and sacrificial efforts made us proud of our fellow Americans. Such compassionate deeds, though extraordinary and inspiring, are expected in the face of such unreal calamity. We probably would want to do the same if put in that kind of position and situation.

Yet, how do we act on a daily basis? Do we treat those with desperate needs compassionately? Do we go places where most don't bother or can't imagine going?

These questions and many more penetrate the superficial layers of our Christianity and jar us back to reality. Jesus desires (and demonstrates) nothing less than for His people to show compassion to others, no matter how unpopular or uncelebrated our actions may be.

In fact, that sort of selfless resolve marked the early church and literally rocked an empire for Christ. These believers in Jesus were the heroes of the first century!

"The types of good works most often mentioned by those who know the actions of the early Christians well are compassion and community. While their undaunted courage proved the point of their commitment, and their consecration to the message offered others something significant to believe in, compassion and community drove early Christianity into the mainstream of life in the empire. These two commodities offered an attractive alternative and an undeniable picture of the love of Jesus. They were the fields upon which the power of Jesus was unleashed. In what was often a loveless, hedonistic world full of gods that didn't love or help, compassion and community met the longings of the human spirit."
—*The Trouble With Jesus*, 112–13.

Questions for Reflection

What do you believe compelled the first Christians to live so selflessly?

_____

_____

_____

How was their culture different from ours? How was it the same?

_____

_____

_____

How do twenty-first-century lifestyles hinder most Christians from acting with the same selflessness that marked the early church?

_____

_____

Read the excerpt on pages 118 and 119 in *The Trouble With Jesus* from the article written in the *New York Times*. Why are these journalist's observations significant?

_____

_____

_____

There were no major media outlets covering the selfless deeds of Christ's followers in the first century. No satellite news coverage broadcasting Christians in action in the leper camps and disease-infested villages. Still, the world took notice and Christ was honored and made known. These first-century Christians were merely following their Master's example:

> In reply Jesus said: "A man was going down from Jerusalem to Jericho, when he fell into the hands of robbers. They stripped him of his clothes, beat him and went away, leaving him half dead. A priest happened to be going down the same road, and when he saw the man, he passed by on the other side. So too, a Levite, when he came to the place and saw him, passed by on the other side. But a Samaritan, as he traveled, came where the man was; and when he saw him, he took pity on him. He went to him and bandaged his wounds, pouring on oil and wine. Then he put the man on his own donkey, took him to an inn and took care of him. The next day he took out two silver coins and gave them to the innkeeper. 'Look after him,' he said, 'and when I return, I will reimburse you for any extra expense you may have.'
>
> "Which of these three do you think was a neighbor to the man who fell into the hands of robbers?"
>
> ≫ LUKE 10:30–36

What would have been some of the surprising elements of Jesus' story to those who heard the parable?

_____

_____

What did Jesus want His listeners to do as a result?

_____

_____

What hindered the other men in the story from showing compassion? What hinders us from showing compassion toward our neighbors?

_____

_____

_____

Compassion in Action

Clearly, having compassionate sentiments is not enough to represent Jesus in a non-Jesus world. Jesus wants us to act when we feel compassion toward those in need. Too often we *feel* compassion, but are never compelled to act.

A LOOK at the BOOK

Luke 7:22

What do these verses teach us about the mission of Jesus on earth? What kind of people does Jesus want us to be concerned about?

_____

_____

_____

Psalm 9:9; Proverbs 14:31

Who were the oppressed of Jesus' day?

_____

_____

Who are the oppressed of our day? How far away from your home do you have to travel to find people who are oppressed and in need of compassion?

_____

_____

_____

James 1:27

Why do you think James mentions widows and orphans? What do these two groups have in common? What do you think James means by "looking after" them?

_____

_____

_____

Do you know any widows or orphans?

_____

_____

Mark 1:40–41

What request did the leper bring to Jesus? What was Jesus' response?

_____

_____

_____

What action followed the emotion of compassion?

_____

_____

Why is that action significant?

_____

_____

What was the result of Jesus' compassionate deed toward this man?

_____

_____

Colossians 3:12

How do we as Christians clothe ourselves with compassion?

_____

_____

James 5:11

Why is this passage significant?

_____

_____

What does it tell us about God and what He expects of His followers?

_____

_____

Now would be a good time to pause and thank the Lord for His mercy and compassion toward us. All we have in Christ is a result of God looking on us in our desperate situation and showing mercy and compassion. Take a moment to thank Him for His compassion.

ACTIONPOINTS

⇨Contact your pastor or local ministry leader and request a list of the widows in your church and community. Then pray about ways to reach out to them, perhaps driving them to the doctor's office, doing some cleaning or grocery shopping, or making sure their yards are kept and sidewalks shoveled in the winter. Some may simply need a friend to talk with from time to time.

⇨Prayerfully consider financially supporting a child orphaned by AIDS in Africa. Check with relief organizations such as *World Vision, Samaritan's Purse,* or *Compassion International* for possibilities.

⇨Befriend someone in your community or local body of believers who is outcast, typically overlooked, or who doesn't fit into the larger crowd.

⇨Consider making regular visits to a local nursing home, orphanage, or hospital to encourage people in those places.

> Lord Jesus, thank You for showing us
> how to love the unlovely around us.
> Thank You for not leaving us as orphans
> and for providing for our needs. May we
> be compassionate toward those in need
> today. In Your merciful name, Amen.

Dear friends, let us love one another, for love comes from God. Everyone who loves has been born of God and knows God. Whoever does not love does not know God, because God is love. This is how God showed his love among us: He sent his one and only Son into the world that we might live through him. This is love: not that we loved God, but that he loved us and sent his Son as an atoning sacrifice for our sins. Dear friends, since God so loved us, we also ought to love one another. No one has ever seen God; but if we love one another, God lives in us and his love is made complete in us.

≫ 1 JOHN 4:7–12 ≪

CHAPTER SEVEN

WELCOME...IN JESUS' NAME

Commitment 4:
Community...Loving for Jesus

The majority of the world's population lives in urban and suburban centers. Half a century ago, millions of Americans left the wide-open spaces of country living for the promise of prosperity and opportunity offered by the large metropolis. American suburbia has become a subculture of modern times. Houses stand at attention, block after block, as far as the eye can see in concentric circles surrounding America's major cities. A strange by-product of urban and suburban living is a palpable isolation that most families maintain from the larger community in which they live. Many families erect six- to eight-foot high fences around the small lots they own to secure some semblance of privacy and safety. A genuine sense of community has been lost to our cell phone-controlled, fenced-in, and commuter-driven culture.

None of that was the case in the first-century church. Community and family was everything—a by-product of God's inaugurating Spirit He poured out on believers at Pentecost (Acts 2). The Christian family of brothers and sisters superceded ties of natural family, blood relations. But even then, viewing brothers and sisters in Christ as the genuine family represented a major shift in culture.

"One of the radical paradigm shifts Jesus introduced into His world was the notion that true family was no longer based on ancestry but on being born into His family. The radical nature of this shift was scandalous in His day. There was no greater point of loyalty in the ancient world than loyalty to one's brother or sister. In fact, loyalty expressed to your siblings was even more intense than loyalty to parents or spouse.

It was clear from the beginning that one of the purposes of Jesus' mission on earth was to establish a new subculture through which salt and light could be dispensed. This new group would be like family. Family—with its mutual commitments, loyal connectedness, common heritage, and familial mind-set—would now be the way that followers of Jesus should view their relationships." — *The Trouble With Jesus*, 127.

Who Are My Brothers and Sisters?

Jesus came to bring a new order to the human race—a radical, transformed subculture that had Him at its center and His followers as His subjects. The community of faith was made up of the body of Christ, disciples of Jesus who loved Him and loved each other with a supernatural love.

Questions for Reflection

What do you think of when you hear the word *community?*

_____

_____

_____

In what ways does technology help or hinder a genuine sense of Christian community?

_____

_____

How would you describe the community in which you live? What one word would you use to describe your community of faith, your church family?

_____

_____

Why do you think Jesus' emphasis on being part of God's family appeared radical to the people of His day?

_____

_____

Why do you believe we insist on maintaining isolated, independent lifestyles?

_____

_____

How does that insistence keep us from experiencing the fullness of what Jesus came to bring?

_____

_____

How does the depth of your loyalty and love toward your earthly family—your parents, brothers and sisters, children and grandchildren—compare to your loyalty and love for your brothers and sisters in Christ?

_____

_____

Why are you more likely to live sacrificially for one group or the other?

_____

_____

The Day That Changed Everything

The book of Acts chronicles the beginning and development of the church, compliments of Luke. Luke was a trained physician and

59

historian as well as a companion of the Apostle Paul. He had remarkable insight into the people and events that marked the beginning of the church. After Jesus had already ascended to heaven, the Holy Spirit came down at Pentecost and transformed a small band of disciples who were praying together. They would never be the same and neither would the rest of the world. Below is an excerpt from the early part of the book of Acts.

> When the day of Pentecost came, they were all together in one place. Suddenly a sound like the blowing of a violent wind came from heaven and filled the whole house where they were sitting. They saw what seemed to be tongues of fire that separated and came to rest on each of them. All of them were filled with the Holy Spirit and began to speak in other tongues as the Spirit enabled them.
>
> They devoted themselves to the apostles' teaching and to the fellowship, to the breaking of bread and to prayer. Everyone was filled with awe, and many wonders and miraculous signs were done by the apostles. All the believers were together and had everything in common. Selling their possessions and goods, they gave to anyone as he had need. Every day they continued to meet together in the temple courts. They broke bread in their homes and ate together with glad and sincere hearts, praising God and enjoying the favor of all the people. And the Lord added to their number daily those who were being saved.
>
> ~ ACTS 2:1–4, 42–47

Make a list of everything that happened after Pentecost.

_____

_____

What kind of power is required to bring about radical changes?

_____

_____

What do you believe is the significance of the tongues of fire resting "on each of them" as Luke describes it?

_____

_____

According to this passage, what happens when believers in Jesus are filled with the Holy Spirit? How are people around them affected?

_____

_____

What does the filling of the Spirit have to do with Christian community?

_____

_____

What does Luke mean by "all the believers were together and had everything in common"?

_____

_____

What do you think God desires of Christians today when it comes to community?

_____

_____

Is your home a place where you and fellow believers could (or already do) gather to find encouragement, support, fellowship, and healing? If not your home, where could (or do) you get together?

_____

_____

_____

You can begin to see how a radical change in perspective is needed for most Christians today. Our lives and our homes remain largely private affairs. Most of us are not naturally inclined to open ourselves up to others and to make our resources and possessions available to the larger body of Christ. Naturally, that is. But *supernaturally* we can! When the Spirit of God takes control and fills us, our attitudes about our possessions and the use of our homes are transformed.

> "Noteworthy to a watching world was the unusual practice of Christians using their own homes as an outstretched hand of hospitality that provided strategic way stations for the gospel." —*The Trouble With Jesus,* 130.

Take a look at several passages of Scripture that demonstrate how first-century Christians used their homes and resources to minister to the needs of the community of faith. Then write a one- or two-word response to each passage.

Acts 4:32–35   **Acts 12:12**

Romans 16:4, 23   **1 Corinthians 16:15, 19**

Colossians 4:5   **Philemon 2–7, 20–22**

John 13:34–35   **Galatians 5:22–26**

John 15:10–12

Clearly, the Bible teaches that Christians are to provide a warm welcome in Jesus' name to a lost and needy world. But we begin with those who have needs in our own family of faith. It's loving one another because Christ loved us first. In the eyes of a watching world, that love melts away the doubt, fear, and skepticism that keep lost people from embracing the truth.

*ACTION*POINTS

Write out your own points of action based on what you've discovered in God's Word. Here is a list of questions to prompt your thinking.

⇨ Is your home a Spirit-controlled lighthouse for the family of faith to find refuge and refreshment?

⇨ Are you and your family known for your hospitality and generosity?

⇨ How might you actively seek to stay aware of the needs of people in your church family and in your community?

⇨ Who benefits from your God-entrusted resources of money, possessions, and time?

⇨ How might you adjust those priorities to comply with God's Word and Jesus' expectations to love others and meet the needs of the family of faith?

⇨ Are you presently involved in ministry? Why or why not? If not, what do you think keeps you from using the gifts God has given you?

⇨ Is the supernatural outflow of your life devoted to serving Christ and meeting the needs of others?

Lord, I realize I've been living too focused on meeting my needs rather than the needs of others. The needs of others are great, both in my church family and in the community around me. Transform my attitudes and adjust my priorities so that I can be obedient to You and give everyone I come in contact with a genuine welcome—in Jesus' name.

63

As Jesus was walking beside the Sea of Galilee, he
saw two brothers, Simon called Peter and his brother
Andrew. They were casting a net into the lake, for
they were fishermen. "Come, follow me," Jesus said,
"and I will make you fishers of men." At once they
left their nets and followed him.

Going on from there, he saw two other brothers,
James son of Zebedee and his brother John. They
were in a boat with their father Zebedee, preparing
their nets. Jesus called them, and immediately they left
the boat and their father and followed him.

≈ MATTHEW 4:18–22 ≈

CHAPTER EIGHT

THE CENTRALITY OF JESUS

Commitment 5:
Consecration . . . Living for Jesus

Well, that's the trouble with Jesus. He demands and deserves absolute devotion and allegiance. He wants those who follow Him to experience the fullness of a relationship with Him, marked by sacrificial obedience and unswerving devotion. Yet the comforts and conveniences the world offers are a strong force to resist. In fact, many Christians prefer a sort of easy-chair Christianity that allows them the benefits of association with Jesus without the cost of full surrender. But Jesus has drawn a line in the sand and challenges us to choose sides. In this non-Jesus world, there's no room for fence-sitting followers.

"If our true identity is that we are first and foremost followers of Jesus, shouldn't it be the first thing on our mind, the first thing on our list? Sometimes I am in groups where John Calvin is quoted more often and with more authority than Jesus or the apostles. To his credit, John Calvin would be embarrassed.

A prevalent obstruction to the centrality and supremacy of Jesus is our preoccupation with ourselves. Why do we keep embarrassing ourselves and Jesus by living lives that are consumed with ourselves—my preferences, my style, my perspective, my plans? If we are followers of Jesus, it is supposed to be all about Him." — *The Trouble With Jesus,* 144–145.

Just like His disciples, Jesus calls us to follow Him too. That requires an undistracted commitment to go where He leads, do what He says, and become what He requires. As we near the end of this study, take some time to reflect on just what that type of commitment really means.

Questions for Reflection

What do you think Jesus expects from us when He calls us to "follow Him"?

_____

_____

_____

_____

In what ways do you think creature comforts and other attractions of our present culture hinder Christians from making a full surrender to God's will?

_____

_____

_____

How do the notions of the "American dream," such as prosperity and success, conflict with Christ's command to follow Him?

_____

_____

_____

How would it have been easier to be a fully devoted follower of Jesus in the first century than it would be in the twenty-first century? How would it have been harder to follow Jesus in the first century?

_____

_____

What does it mean to be consecrated to Jesus?

_____

_____

Follow Me!

In today's evangelical culture, peculiar emphasis on developing well-trained, visionary, and skillful leaders has emerged. Interestingly, Jesus did not call His disciples to *lead*. He called them to *follow*. What our world and the church needs today are not more leaders but genuine followers willing to take up a cross and follow Jesus.

> "True followers stay in hot pursuit of Jesus, who promised that He is a rewarder of them that diligently seek Him. As we become more like Him and passionately pursue Him, it becomes apparent that He is leading us to the needs of people who are lost in their non-Jesus world. It's no wonder that Jesus said to His disciples, 'Follow me, and I will make you fishers of men' (Matthew 4:19)."
> —*The Trouble With Jesus*, 149.

Peter and Andrew and both Zebedee brothers were used to a certain independence that came from working in the family business. No supervisors, no clocking in and out at some factory, no reports owed to shareholders. They pursued their livelihood with the gusto and passion that most entrepreneurs do.

Do you think it was a coincidence that Jesus' first disciples were fishermen by trade? Why or why not?

_____

_____

How would you explain their willingness to walk away from independence and follow a transient prophet from Nazareth?

_____

_____

What do you think might have been the financial impact of their decisions to leave everything and follow Jesus?

_____

_____

What might have been the emotional and relational cost of such no-looking-back decisions?

_____

_____

Upon Christ's invitation to follow, both sons of Zebedee left their father and their boats. Why do you think Matthew included the emphasis on leaving their father and their boats?

_____

_____

Following Jesus means two things. First, imitating Him. Second, pursuing Him. The New Testament describes and prescribes both. Read the passages below and write out in the space provided what each passage teaches about following Jesus.

Imitating Jesus

JOHN 8:12: *When Jesus spoke again to the people, he said, "I am the light of the world. Whoever follows me will never walk in darkness, but will have the light of life."*

_____

_____

MATTHEW 11:28–29: *Come to me, all you who are weary and burdened, and I will give you rest. Take my yoke upon you and learn from me, for I am gentle and humble in heart, and you will find rest for your souls. For my yoke is easy and my burden is light.*

JOHN 4:33–34: *Then his disciples said to each other, "Could someone have brought him food?"*

"My food," said Jesus, "is to do the will of him who sent me and to finish his work."

JOHN 7:16–18: *Jesus answered, "My teaching is not my own. It comes from him who sent me. If anyone chooses to do God's will, he will find out whether my teaching comes from God or whether I speak on my own. He who speaks on his own does so to gain honor for himself, but he who works for the honor of the one who sent him is a man of truth."*

JOHN 13:12–14: *When he had finished washing their feet, he put on his clothes and returned to his place. "Do you understand what I have done for you?" he asked them. "You call me 'Teacher' and 'Lord,' and rightly so, for that is what I am. Now that I, your Lord and Teacher, have washed your feet, you also should wash one another's feet."*

PHILIPPIANS 2:5–8: *Your attitude should be the same as that of Christ Jesus: Who, being in very nature God, did not consider equality with God something to be grasped, but made himself nothing, taking the very nature of a servant, being made in human likeness. And being found in appearance as a man, he humbled himself and became obedient to death—even death on a cross!*

_____

_____

Pursuing Jesus

MATTHEW 10:37–39: *Anyone who loves his father or mother more than me is not worthy of me; anyone who loves his son or daughter more than me is not worthy of me; and anyone who does not take his cross and follow me is not worthy of me. Whoever finds his life will lose it, and whoever loses his life for my sake will find it.*

_____

_____

MATTHEW 15:22–28: *A Canaanite woman from that vicinity came to him, crying out, "Lord, Son of David, have mercy on me! My daughter is suffering terribly from demon-possession."*

Jesus did not answer a word. So his disciples came to him and urged him, "Send her away, for she keeps crying out after us."

He answered, "I was sent only to the lost sheep of Israel." The woman came and knelt before him. "Lord, help me!" she said.

He replied, "It is not right to take the children's bread and toss it to their dogs."

"Yes, Lord," she said, "but even the dogs eat the crumbs that fall from their masters' table."

Then Jesus answered, "Woman, you have great faith! Your request is granted."

_____

_____

JOHN 4:13–14: *Jesus answered, "Everyone who drinks this water will be thirsty again, but whoever drinks the water I give him will never thirst. Indeed the water I give him will become in him a spring of water welling up to eternal life."*

_____

_____

PHILIPPIANS 3:7–8: *But whatever was to my profit I now consider loss for the sake of Christ. What is more, I consider everything a loss compared to the surpassing greatness of knowing Christ Jesus my Lord, for whose sake I have lost all things.*

ACTIONPOINTS

Finish the following sentences as honestly as possible.

⇨From this day on I give Jesus my . . .

⇨The thing(s) in my life keeping me from following Jesus is (are) . . .

⇨To Jesus, my Lord and King, I surrender . . .

Surrendering fully to Jesus is the key to beginning a life that effectively impacts your world for Him. Now it's your turn. Touched by Jesus, you are commissioned to use your life to bless an often-hostile world with the undeniable reality of the power and presence of His love.

This is our day as Christians. We are His salt and light. It is our destiny and privilege! Seize the opportunity to stand up for Jesus in our non-Jesus world!

It's time to draw the line...
and show the world that Jesus is the way!

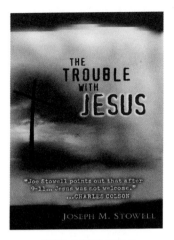

ISBN: 0-8024-1093-6

The world has no time or space for Jesus; in fact, society finds the claims of Christ too demanding and scandalously intolerant. So how do followers of Christ stand for Jesus in today's world? Dr. Joseph Stowell helps readers understand the non-Christian influence and gives them guidance on how to reach a hostile world.

My good friend, Joe Stowell, points out that after 9/11, God was—at least temporarily— back. But, in the mushy ecumenism that followed the attacks, Jesus was not welcome. Rather than indulge in hand-wringing, Stowell analyzes the problem and goes on to provide wise, practical principles for making Jesus known in our challenging day and in our jaded culture.
> **Chuck Colson**, founder, Prison Ministries, author, speaker

In *The Trouble with Jesus*, Joe Stowell exposes the emptiness of the post 9/11 American spirituality as paganism dressed up in the clothes of patriotic unity. The book is a "must-read" if you call yourself a Christian. As your eyes read the words, the ears of your heart will hear the clear trumpet call of the King as He rallies His troops, challenging each of us to lift high the banner of His Name!
> **Anne Graham Lotz**, AnGel Ministries

MOODY
PUBLISHERS
THE NAME YOU CAN TRUST.

1-800-678-6928 www.MoodyPublishers.org

The Trouble with Jesus Bible Study Team

ACQUIRING EDITOR
Greg Thornton

COPY EDITOR
Ali Childers

BACK COVER COPY
Elizabeth Cody Newenhuyse

COVER DESIGN
Ragont Design

COVER PHOTO
Digital Stock

INTERIOR DESIGN
Ragont Design

PRINTING AND BINDING
Color House

The typeface for the text of this book is
Sabon